DO YOU REALLY WANT TO MEET TRICERATOPS?

BY ANNETTE BAY PIMENTEL • ILLUSTRATED BY DANIELE FABBRI

AMICUS ILLUSTRATED and AMICUS INK
are published by Amicus
P.O. Box 1329, Mankato, MN 56002
www.amicuspublishing.us

EDITOR: Rebecca Glaser
DESIGNER: Kathleen Petelinsek

LIBRARY OF CONGRESS CATALOGING-IN-PUBLICATION DATA
Names: Pimentel, Annette Bay, author. | Fabbri, Daniele,
   illustrator.
Title: Do you really want to meet triceratops? / by Annette
   Bay Pimentel ; illustrated by Daniele Fabbri.
Other titles: Do you really want to meet...?
Description: Mankato, MN : Amicus Illustrated/Amicus Ink,
   [2018] | Series: Do you really want to meet a dinosaur? |
   Audience: K to grade 3. | Includes bibliographical references.
Identifiers: LCCN 2016054921 (print) | LCCN 2016056304
   (ebook) | ISBN 9781681511153 (library binding) | ISBN
   9781681521404 (pbk.) | ISBN 9781681512051 (e-book)
Subjects: LCSH: Triceratops—Juvenile literature. |
   Dinosaurs—Juvenile literature.
Classification: LCC QE862.065 P565 2018 (print) | LCC
   QE862.065 (ebook) | DDC 567.915/8—dc23
LC record available at https://lccn.loc.gov/2016054921

Printed in the United States of America
HC 10 9 8 7 6 5 4
PB 10 9 8 7 6 5 4 3 2 1

ABOUT THE AUTHOR
Annette Bay Pimentel lives in Moscow, Idaho with her family.
She doesn't have a time machine, so she researches the
past at the library. She writes about what happened a
long time ago in nonfiction picture books like *Mountain Chef*
(2016, Charlesbridge). You can visit her online at
www.annettebaypimentel.com.

ABOUT THE ILLUSTRATOR
Daniele Fabbri was born in Ravenna, Italy, in 1978. He
graduated from Istituto Europeo di Design in Milan,
Italy, and started his career as a cartoon animator,
storyboarder, and background designer for animated
series. He has worked as a freelance illustrator since 2003,
collaborating with advertising agencies and international
publishers, including many books for Amicus.

Your pet chameleon looks just like a tiny Triceratops. A real Triceratops was as big as an elephant. Its horns were 3 feet (1 m) long! You know that already? And you still want to meet a real Triceratops?

You have a time machine, right? Set it for 66 million years ago. That's during the Cretaceous Period, before dinosaurs went extinct. Triceratops fossils have been found across western North America. Many were found in Montana. That's a good place to start.

66 mil YEARS

Western North America was warm and wet back then, and you've landed near a river. Watch closely and you might see turtles, snails, lizards, and even mammals.

But you probably won't find a Triceratops
near the river. Time to start hiking.

What's that smell? It's a giant pile of dinosaur poop! Someday it could turn into a rocky fossil.

Scientists will learn what dinosaurs ate by studying it. Maybe the dinosaur that made that pile is nearby. Yes! There it is!

From here you can see it eating. *Crunch!* With its sharp beak, Triceratops can chomp branches too tough for other dinosaurs to eat. Inside its mouth are 800 strong teeth for chewing.

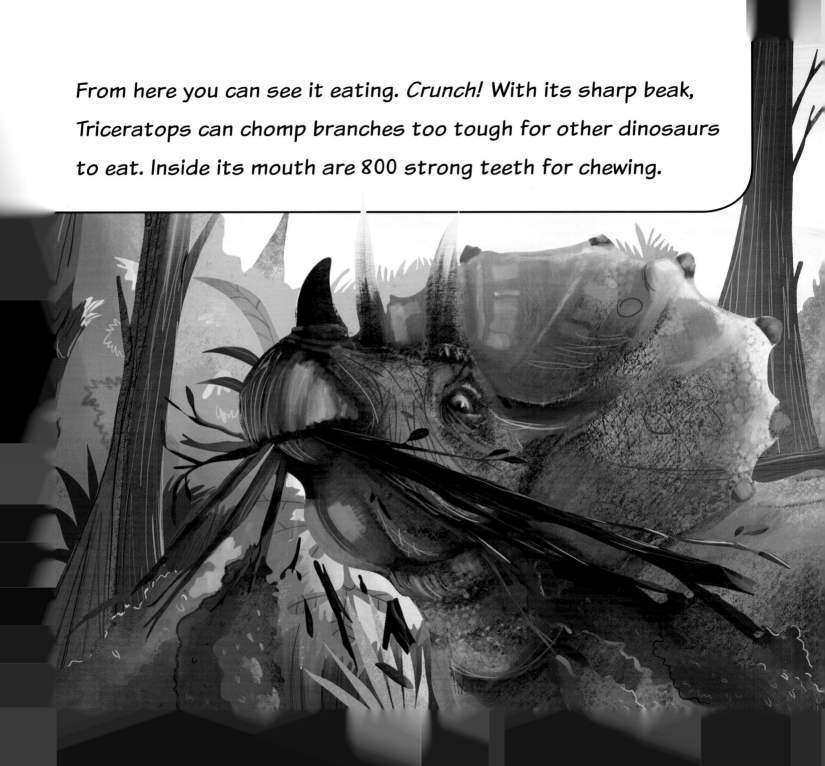

What's that moving? The dinosaur isn't by itself.

There are three Triceratops together! Older Triceratops wander alone. So these must be young. You can also tell by their horns. Look. The horns above their eyes curve backward. As they grow, their horns will grow straight and then curve forward. Maybe you can find an adult, too. Keep hiking.

Whoa! There's a T. rex. Stay low and still. T. rex was the fiercest predator in the Cretaceous Period. It's looking at something. Can you tell what?

It's another Triceratops! See how its horns point forward? That tells you it's an adult. It's bigger than the others you saw, too. What will T. rex do?

Charge! T. rex attacks, but Triceratops stands its ground. It's big. It has a large bony frill around its neck. And of course, it has those horns!

The T. rex changes its mind. It leaves to find something easier to catch.

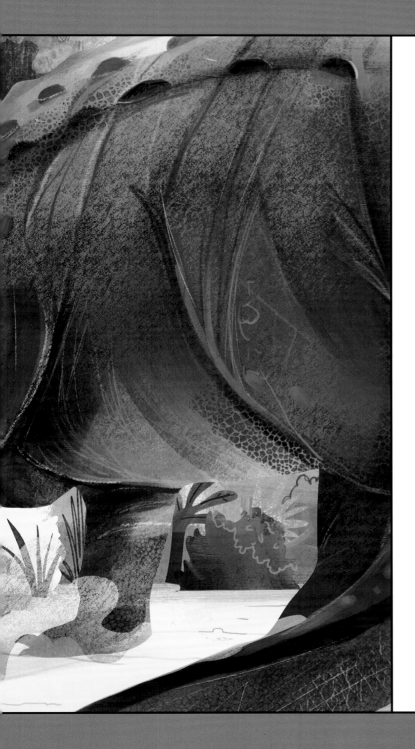

Now Triceratops has a different problem. Another adult Triceratops wants to fight. Usually adults stay by themselves. Maybe these two both want the same territory. Maybe they're fighting over a mate. They've locked horns!

This is no fake fight. Triceratops really get injured in these battles. You don't want to get caught in the action. Time to leave this prehistoric horned wonder and head home to your pet chameleon, your own horned wonder.

WHERE HAVE TRICERATOPS FOSSILS BEEN FOUND?

GLOSSARY

Cretaceous Period—The time between 145.5 million and 65.5 million years ago. Dinosaurs lived during this time.

extinct—No longer existing anywhere in the world.

fossil—A bone or other trace of an animal from millions of years ago, preserved as rock.

frill—A fan-shaped bone on a dinosaur's neck.

mammal—A warm-blooded animal that has hair or fur; they usually give birth to live young.

predator—An animal that hunts and eats other animals for food.

territory—An area that is occupied and defended by an animal.

T. rex—A dinosaur predator that lived at the same time as Triceratops.

AUTHOR'S NOTE

Too bad for us, time machines aren't real. But all of the details about Triceratops in this book are based on research by scientists who study fossils. For example, in 2015 scientists studied Triceratops teeth. They realized that the teeth got sharper and sharper as Triceratops chewed, until the teeth were as sharp as knives. So this plant-eater could eat plants other dinosaurs couldn't chew! New dinosaur discoveries are made every year. Look up the books and websites below to learn more.

READ MORE

Alpert, Barbara. *Triceratops*. Mankato, Minn.: Amicus, 2014.

Holtz, Thomas R. *Digging for Triceratops: A Discovery Timeline*. North Mankato, Minn.: Capstone, 2015.

WEBSITES

DINOSAUR DAYS: TRICERATOPS
http://www.dinosaurdays.com/cretaceous_triceratops.html
Watch an animated video about Triceratops.

DINOSAURS: NATIONAL GEOGRAPHIC KIDS
http://kids.nationalgeographic.com/explore/nature/dinosaurs/
Compare sizes of dinosaurs, meet paleontologists, and more.

Every effort has been made to ensure that these websites are appropriate for children. However, because of the nature of the Internet, it is impossible to guarantee that these sites will remain active indefinitely or that their contents will not be altered.